What Others Are Saying

"Amazing! Full of useful information for all of us."
-Michael Ioannou, Author

"At last! A book-guide for every modern seller written with clarity and honesty by an experienced seller and businessman."
-Phillip Stagos, Executive Director, Vais Corp

"The new perception of sales has become a reality a long time ago. It's high time we were adapted to it."
-George Stavridis, Sales Manager, Argocom Corp

"Win On Sale, A New Perception Of Sale And Its 22 Basic Principles Or A Guide For The Modern Seller gives us something that is difficult to be found: how the market works today and how sales can lead us to what every businessman looks for, in other words to results."
-Andrew Christou, CEO, Intertext Corp

"A simple, brief and different book that will help us to improve what we have already been doing and be able to survive in the difficult economic environment of our modern society."

-John Spiridis, Professional Seller, Pronet Corp

Win On Sale

A New Perception Of Sale And Its 22 Basic
Principles

Or

A Guide For The Modern Seller

Christos Stilianidis

Visit author page at

www.win-on-sale.com

ISBN: 978-960-93-4225-4

The present book is dedicated to all those who believe they can be successful and are persistent in achieving that goal.

Contents

Introduction

About four years ago, one of the students in the Faculty of Business Administration of the University of my city asked me to give her an interview concerning sales for a project that she was conducting during that time period. During the interview, I was asked many questions as far as selling ways that I used, the way of presenting and sampling products as well as the way I dealt with my clients' objections.

I was really surprised by the attention she paid to "persuasion" and to the way we could reach the final result through the use of persuasion. It was the moment when I realized the following: theory regarding sales has left behind in comparison with reality. We no more need persuasion in order to sell.

We do not need to "deal with" or "manage" a single objection expressed by our clients. In today's modern consuming society, things have completely changed. Selling is a procedure conducted on its own. The seller has no longer the need to persuade as it was in the past. The modern seller is the person who facilitates consumer to do the thing that loves the most: to buy.

Hence, the first chapter includes this new perception concerning sales while the second chapter contains all modern techniques based on this perception as well as how these techniques can be adapted to each one of us. Finally, in chapter three we will learn about the 22 Basic Principles regarding sales with the application of which we will be transformed from simple people working on sales to Professional Sellers.

Chapter One

A New Perception of Sale

Capacity Throughout a Day

Every region - such as a quarter, a city, a prefecture, a state etc - as far as external sales are concerned, has its own "capacity", just like the number of people that get into a shop or a department store every day - regarding internal sales - is characterized by certain "capacity", based on the store's size. What does this mean? It means that there is a number of potential clients living in this particular area or concerning the total of people who enter the store and feel ready to buy something.

There are two main basic rules regarding sales. The first - empirical - rule states that: "three out of ten potential clients decide to buy". Even though it seems to be unbelievable, this rule is valid and it is confirmed on a daily basis. As we stated above, capacity characterizing a region or a total of persons that will enter a store is reflected in this particular rule. What does this practically mean? It refers to the three following:

1. A sale achievement is an issue of statistics. On average, three out of ten people that we will meet at our store will decide to buy. It further means that in any case, there will be sales on a daily basis. We simply do not know who these three

out of ten potential clients will eventually decide to buy something.

2. We already know in advance that we are not interested in making sales to all potential clients that we will see in a day! We focus on selling to those people belonging to the region's "capacity" or to the "capacity" of those people that are about to enter our store this particular day.

3. Hence, every day we aim at getting in contact with as many clients as possible in order to explore every day's "capacity" and achieve more sales.

The second fundamental rule regarding sales, which in fact supports and completes the first one, is Pareto's principle - or the rule of 80/20 - according to which: 80% of sales come from 20% of people we will see. In fact, this particular principle confirms the first rule since it supports that most of our sales will derive from 20% (on average) of the total number of persons that we will meet in a day.

According to those two rules as well as to all the above mentioned, we realize that the main issue for all of us who work or will work on sales is not whether we achieve sales on a daily basis - according to those rules stated above, we will achieve sales in any case - but how we will eventually find out who are those clients that belong to that day's capacity so as to increase our sales.

We Do Not Need to Convince Anybody. We Have Already Been Convinced for Years

For years, selling has been totally identified with persuasion, a fact that still exists. We all think that a seller has to "persuade" those persons with whom he will get in contact with so as to buy things from him, in other words, the seller has to "pitch" his products or services. Therefore, most people are negative towards the idea of working on sales. This idea still exists and it is maintained by many people who work on sales and by many books written on sales that really pay too much attention to the way we could manage and deal with clients' objections. All the above stated share the clear opinion that a seller should persuade his client during selling procedure.

This kind of sales model has been completely modified. The seller does not have to persuade anyone. Why? Because we have already been persuaded for years through the advertisements and the marketing promoted by television, the magazines, the newspapers, the radio and the internet. Hence, mass media have already convinced us all these years that our life without buying, changes, new things and lifestyle is not too much worthy according to the concept of our modern, consuming society: "I buy things, hence I exist" or even better "I do not buy things, hence I do not exist!!!".

No matter how incredible does it seem to be, it is hard for us NOT TO buy. Modern man is so much saturated since a very young age by the need to buy that he can no more resist to the temptation of a new purchase. Hence, the percentage of those purchases made in order to cover our real needs is minimal. All the above mentioned are also supported by Second Parkinson's Law, according to which: "The higher our income is, the more our expenditure tend to be equal to it". In other words, it means that no matter how much does our income increase, we will always have tendency to spend money!!!

Example: Is it random the fact that each time we feel sorrow, we go for shopping therapy? Is it random the fact that our children are constantly asking for new toys even though their rooms are full of them? Is it random the fact that as soon as they get a new toy, they leave it because they have just satisfied their need for getting something new? Is it random that as soon as we buy a new car, it is already considered to be old because there comes the next car model? All these things are certainly not coincidental.

Moreover, it is not random at all the fact that during periods of economic crisis such as the one we live in today, most of us face psychological problems or even depression. Why? Because we are not able to practice the sport related to our purchasing and consuming addiction which we used to do all these years. We cannot be self-confirmed through all these things that we buy not only for ourselves but also for our beloved persons. We feel that we are left behind the development of the society, fashion and the lifestyle through which all ads presented at all means of communication try to influence us in a subconscious way.

Therefore, there are plenty of reasons for which a potential customer would like to make a purchase from us. Maybe, he wants to feel self-confirmed, maybe because he is disappointed with his current cooperation, maybe because he trusted us, because he thinks that our prices are better in comparison to others, maybe because he believes that the value of our product or service is better in comparison to the one already has.

Moreover, another reason is the fact that he is constantly interested in finding bargains, because he searches for some other suggestions to his problem or because he liked us, because he thinks that this purchase will promote his lifestyle, because he thinks that our product is a status symbol, because he wants to please another person, because he does not wish to be left behind a general trend existing around him or characterizing our society at present time etc.

Thus, by applying a simple, repetitive procedure, we discover every day which one among our potential clients with whom we get in contact, is ready to buy or feel the need to make a purchase. This procedure is called the "sales procedure".

The Price Of a Product Is Different From Its Value

There is a general perception that a low price is necessary for a product or service to be sold. In other words, we believe that in case a product or service is not very cheap, selling prospects to a wider public do not exist. Is this true?

Firstly, we have to separate the price of a product or service from its value. A product's price is determined by several factors and it means for the consumer how much money will finally pay in order to buy this product. A product's value is defined by the money the consumer will pay in comparison to benefits derived from this product. We have already analyzed the fact that all purchases we make nowadays are directly connected to multiple benefits derived from them. Hence, the price itself is nothing but a simple number.

Example: How will we characterize a T-shirt whose cost is 17$ in comparison to another whose cost is 8$? Will it be expensive or cheap? And if we compare it to another whose cost is 35$? The main issue according to which we will conclude that this T-shirt is cheap or expensive is what the benefits that will offer to us are. If we think that this T-shirt is drub and shoddy then we will probably consider it to be expensive while if we think that it is stylish then we will see that it makes us looking brighter or ten years younger. So in this case, it's a bargain!!!

Hence, the value of a product or service is the factor that finally defines whether this particular product is expensive or cheap for the modern consumer. In case the money paid by the consumer are not equal to the benefits that he will receive by the product, he considers that the product is expensive, in other words he believes that he pays too much money and he receives very few benefits. In case the benefits offered to the consumer by the purchase of our product or service exceeds the money that he will offer to buy it, he considers that the product is cheap.

Thus, we buy both designer clothes or not. We also buy cars of low, medium or high engine capacity. We also consume both cheap wines and more expensive whiskeys. We get out for a cup of coffee but we also get out for lunch or dinner or we go to nightclubs where we spend more money etc...

Thus, we must be aware of the following:

1. It is possible that we consider a product to be cheap during a specific time period while the

same product in the same price may appear expensive to us during another period of time. This also happens because we characterize products as cheap or expensive in comparison to our income, psychology and emotional state in a particular time period.

2. Prices constantly change. We will always be cheaper in comparison to some people as well as more expensive from some others and this fact changes constantly without being able to control or be aware of it. So, it is very likely that during a given period of time we will be more expensive in comparison to one of our competitors while another time period we will be cheaper.

3. In modern market, each company usually represents many products. Thus, many times we will be cheaper concerning some products in comparison to a particular competitor while at the same time we may be more expensive regarding other products and in comparison to the same competitor.

4. In any case, every day some potential customers may think that we are expensive concerning some or all of our products and some others may

consider that we are cheap concerning the same products!!!

Hence, we realize that the price is a totally subjective matter for each consumer and that when we refer to a product's price, in fact we talk about the value that this products has for us and according to its value we reach the conclusion that this product is either cheap or expensive.

Not Everybody Thinks the Way We Do

Let me say it in a different way. Not everybody buys things the way we do and not everybody reacts the way we would probably do in case of a purchase or a suggestion made by a seller so as to make his product "known" to us. Many times, our personal beliefs regarding a particular situation impede our effort to take part in this situation by believing that since we think that way, probably the majority of population will share the same opinion.

Example: It is very likely that we do not like sellers to call us and inform us about their products (telemarketing) and probably our reaction towards this situation will be negative. This does not mean that all people in our city react in the same way as we do. It just means that this is our reaction. Hence, the fact that we do not like telemarketing does not mean that other people will feel the same because it is very possible that another person who does not have much free time feels flattered by that phone contact and the fact that he is informed about new products or services!

Do you know what the biggest complaint of modern consumer is? The fact that he does not have any free time. I was with a colleague at a store that was next to a bookstore and the owner said that he had no free time to go to the bookstore to take a look at the books! Moreover, a businessman working at a company next to a mobile telephone store claimed that he had no free time to go and take a look at the new mobile telephone programs! Of course, they were both my clients.

Let's not make generalizations based on our personal perceptions. These perceptions are just personal and concern ourselves!

Chapter Two

The Sales Techniques

The Sales Procedure: a Simple, Repetitive Procedure

The sales procedure is really very simple. Like all other procedures that take place in our daily life such as driving, the sales procedure seems to be difficult for us only in the very first time when we try to learn all these new things that we should put into practice.

Day after day, this kind of procedure is finally done automatically and it turns out to be a simple, repetitive procedure that we constantly apply again and again to any new potential customer. Through this procedure we discover those customers that feel ready to make a purchase.

The sales procedure is just one. However, it includes stages that differentiate from one another regarding the sale we have to make, in other words external, internal sale or telemarketing. Let's focus on each case separately.

External Sale Procedure

Nowadays, external sales are the advantage of all enterprises and they are our best friends in periods of crisis. How many external sellers an enterprise has got and how well they have realized what they do, plays a very important role even - sometimes - for the enterprise's survival.

As far as external sales are concerned, we do not wait for the customer to come to us but we go to the customer (at his store, his office, his enterprise, his house). This procedure is done as follows:

1. The most well-known way concerning the conduct of external sales is fixing a phone appointment with the customer. In this case, the customer not only knows when we will come at his place but he is also informed about the reason we will visit him. Of course, every day we try to arrange as many appointments as possible so as to get in contact with as many potential customers as possible.

2. Then, we have the "door to door" way. In this case, there is no former information of those persons we will get in contact with. Usually and for a particular time period - from a day to one

month - we work at a particular region such as a district, a city or a state and we aim at visiting as many potential customers as possible.

There is a substantive difference between external or distant and internal sales. In the first two cases, we are the persons that create customer's curiosity for our products or services while in the case of internal sales, most potential customers, always according to the capacity stated above, have already realized their desire or need to make this purchase and given this fact, they come at our store.

External sales method

Before we start the sales procedure, we put into practice the method according to which we will proceed:

1. Every day, we get in contact with as many potential clients as possible so as to cover as much as possible the region's capacity where we work.

2. The first visit to each potential customer is the "seeding", in other words the fact that the customer gets in contact with something different from what he has seen so far such as another or similar product, another cooperator,

other prices, another service, other expectations etc.

3. The second visit to the customer, after a settled time period - for example after a week - is the "harvest" (the well-known follow up). We go to head those seeds that we have already sowed during our first visit. However, in any case, either it is our first visit or our second one, we apply all stages of external sales knowing that almost 60% - 70% of our sales - according to our product or service - is fixed from our first visit. The follow up procedure will be described in detail in another chapter of the present book.

However, our first concern is to arrange a sale from our first visit.

The stages of external sales
Stage one: The entrance

External sale begins just when we enter the place where our potential customer is. First of all we have to kindly introduce ourselves and describe what are company is and which the product or service we sell is.

Tips:

1. We get in with a smile on our face. The power of smiling is incredibly strong and unique.

2. We introduce ourselves though handshaking even though we may know our potential customer personally.

3. We always address to our customer formally except in case our customer says that we can be on first-name terms with him.

4. We kindly accept every offer for a cup of coffee, refreshment, glass of water etc.

5. We never forget that the first three minutes of our conversation with the client are the most important concerning the impression we will make to the person we address to as well as that the impression made will almost never be forgotten by the customer.

6. In case our potential customer does not have any free time during that moment or he is too busy, we kindly ask him: "Could I come some other time?" or "Is it convenient for you if we settle an appointment around 2:00 pm?" or "I will come back again a little bit later" etc.

Stage Two: Sampling

A) Products

After the conversation has begun and we have presented the aim of this visit, the first thing we should do is to get our dossier including images of our product. Then we put it on the customer's desk while we continue to describe our product. At this particular stage, we aim at increasing the curiosity of our potential customer concerning our product, in other words we aim at making him focus on the product we sell. We refer to the product's features, what it can offer and most of all we highlight the benefits the customer will have by using this product.

At the same time, we continue with the product's sampling either through leaflets or through the product itself (if there is the possibility of carrying the product with us). Our goal focuses on the participation not only of the hearing but of all other senses of the customer - mainly of vision and touch - since the latter will form the customer's final opinion.

In other words, we have to satisfy the need of the customer to see the product, touch it and feel that it belongs to him. Meanwhile, we continue to refer to the different features of the products and mainly to the benefits that the customer will receive through the use of the product.

B) Services

A service sampling is done through the lists and tables that we carry with us making the potential customer realize through facts and numbers, the benefit he will receive if he uses this kind of service, namely how he can earn money in comparison to what he loses now that he does not use our service.

Stage three: Questions - Objections

At this stage and after a successful entrance and sampling, the customer is already interested in our product or service and there is a suspicion in his mind that he could be profited by it. At this stage the customer usually begins to ask questions about the product, its usefulness, about our company etc. He may have objections regarding the effectiveness of the product or service, our service, our company as well as the product's price etc.

In reality, the fact that the customer may have objections proves to us two important things: his past along with his fears. Objections show us what already had happened to the customer during his former attempts to buy something. He does not want this to happen again and he warns us about it.

Because of many bad experiences in the past, the customer has lost his trust both towards products and people since he probably believes that the value of products that he bought in the past, namely the price he paid to have them in comparison to the benefits he would receive by the use of the product, was not the one it should really be. His fears are not baseless. Let's not forget that nowadays, neither all people are faithful nor all products or services are always those the sellers are proud of.

We are never opposed to any objections expressed by the potential customer face to face. He has the right to have objections. However, we try to gain his lost trust and we are separated from all former experiences of the potential customer by supporting our product or service as well as our company so as the client understands that his fears have to do only with his so far experiences and we are there to ensure him for what we say to him.

Hence, we realize that any objections expressed by the potential customer are more a "crisis of trust" towards products and people of nowadays than real objections concerning this particular product or service.

Stage four: The final stage

This is the final stage of the external sales procedure where we finally realize whether the potential customer that we have met feels the "need" or a "strong desire", after the completion of this procedure, to buy our product or service. The above stated will be obvious in case the potential customer asks us the following questions:

1. What is the product's price?
2. What is the cost of the enrolment?
3. What is it necessary to be done in order to become a subscriber?
4. How much does it cost?
5. Is there any kind of arrangement that you offer?
6. How can I have it?
7. Is there any kind of procedure that we should follow?
8. How many days are needed for the product's delivery? etc.

This is exactly the "zero point", the time when we realize that the person standing opposite to us is really interested in our product or service. Our immediate reaction is to take the order form or the application form or the forms including the modes of payment concerning our product while saying that:

1. The procedure needed for someone to become a subscriber is very simple; we simply complete this application form...
2. The mode of payment concerning the product is very simple...

3. There are two modes of payment, cash or by cheque...

4. The present arrangement is the following...
   Finally, we conclude decisively:

1. Do you want to see the whole procedure in practice?

2. Shall we proceed?

3. I will need your personal data...

4. Let's begin with your first and last name...

5. Is your full name Ethan Arthur?

6. Tell me the personal data you wish the invoice to be issued...

7. Is it convenient to you to receive the product tomorrow? Etc.

At this point, we have the so-called "Aggressive agreement closing" of a sale with which we lead our potential customer to the final closing of the agreement.

The person included in a region's capacity during that day will finally proceed to the closing of the agreement. The person that is not included in the region's capacity during that particular day will not make any questions - in most cases - regarding the price of our product or service and the way he can obtain them.

Tips

1. In case after an aggressive closing of the sale we find out that the potential customer still hesitates, in other words he does not know whether he wants to proceed with a purchase or not, this means that his desire to buy the product is still not strong enough so as to proceed to the closing of the agreement. In this case it is probable that the stage of sampling was not successfully completed and therefore we help him to decide by repeating the three last stages and focusing mainly on the stage of sampling while describing once more the product's features and highlighting the benefits that will arise from the use of the product. Finally, we conclude with the aggressive closing of the sale. In most cases, the potential customer will finally proceed to the closing of the agreement.

2. It is very possible that the potential customer will need some time in order to take his final decision. In this case, we fix a new appointment at a particular date with the customer after a settled time period - such as five to six days - so as to make our second visit to the customer and reach our final result.

3. We never forget that the customer is not mainly interested in the features of our product or service but in the benefits he will gain from it and not only in the narrow sense - namely, the economic benefits - but as we have just said, in all forms of benefits such as self-confirmation, emotional satisfaction, new lifestyle etc. Hence, we mainly focus on the benefits arising from the features of the product.

4. "Firstly we sell the product to ourselves and then to the customer". In fact, we put into practice the sales procedure to ourselves, in other words as if were the potential customer at that particular moment. If we feel satisfied and completed as a customer, then our customer will feel exactly the same. If we feel satisfied by the way we have conducted the procedure of sampling and by what we will say, then the customer will feel exactly the same. If we feel satisfied and completed by the whole procedure of sale and if we believe that we are be ready to proceed to a final agreement, then we will have no fear to proceed to a sales closing since in this case the customer will also feel satisfied and completed.

To Follow Up

As we stated above, it is likely that after the completion of the sale procedure with the potential customer, the latter will need some time in order to take his final decision. In this case, we fix along a new appointment at a particular date with the customer after a settled time period of five to six days so as to make our second visit to the customer and reach our final result.

After reminding him who we are and helping him remember the whole situation, we start once more the sale procedure from the very beginning as if it were the first time that we meet the customer. Hence, we take advantage of a second opportunity with this particular customer. If we finally succeed in the sale procedure - through repeating the whole procedure - then we will reach our goal too.

In case we do not reach an agreement and make sure that the potential customer still hesitates in proceeding to a purchase or cooperation, we can proceed with a second follow up. However, it is up to us. We have to count on all different "information" that the customer offer to us during the whole conversation with him regarding how much he is finally interested in our product or service or not and how much we would really like to place this particular customer among our clientele. However, during the second and last follow up to which we will proceed, we should receive a clear answer about whether the customer is finally interested in having cooperation with us.

But, according to most cases, the more we move away from our first visit, the less the possibilities that we reach a final agreement with this potential customer are.

Internal Sale Procedure

As we have already stated in a former paragraph, in case of internal sale, most of our potential customers that will get into our store or our office would like or feel the need to make a purchase. Hence, the change of the existing desire to a real need for buying is definitely easier and if it is carried out by following the right steps, we will reach astonishing results.

The internal sale technique

The technique used in cases of internal sales is simple: we try to get in contact with all customers that get into our store so as to take full advantage of the day's capacity.

The stages of internal sales
Stage one: The customer's entrance

Internal sales procedure begins at that moment when the potential customer enters our store or enterprise. Our first reaction is to move towards him and ask him politely:

"Good morning, how can I help you?" The answers that we will receive to this question are usually the following:

1. "I am looking for a particular product..." or "I am looking for..." or "I am interested in buying..." etc. As soon as we get this kind of answer, we begin with the second stage of sale.

2. The customer may say "I would like to take a look" or something like this or he may give no answer. In this case we give the customer some free time to put his thoughts and desires in order and then we come back and ask him: "Have you found anything satisfactory?" If the customer gives us a positive answer, then we proceed with the second stage of sale.

    In case the customer gives a negative answer, then we say: "Do you prefer this type of product or that one?" while trying to help him make up his mind, or "If you ask me, I would propose..." or "For the time being, this product is on offer. Take a look at it..." and we finally lead the whole situation to the next stage of sales. In case the potential customer still answers that he simply wants to take a look at our products and he does not look for something in particular, this means that he does not belong to the customer's capacity characterizing this particular day, in other words he does not wish to make a purchase, hence we continue with our next potential customer.

Tips

1. We never forget the power of smiling.
2. We "make" the customer's day and we are always polite towards him. Be sure that you have not forgotten it.

Stage two: Sampling
A) Products

During the second stage, as in external sales, we have the process of sampling concerning the product chosen by the customer or suggested by us. In case of internal sales we have the great advantage of carrying the product with us. We mainly care about the participation of all customer's senses in the process of sampling.

We should show him the product so as to touch it, feel it and smell it. The customer should feel the product as if it belonged to him; we should try it on him - if this is possible - so as to facilitate the change of his desire to make a purchase to a real need for this particular product.

B) Services

In this case we never forget to treat the customer a cup of coffee or a refreshment while we use all our material along with data, tables and numbers so as the customer realizes the profit he will receive as soon as he buys our service.

Stage three: The final stage

As in case of external sales, this is the final stage of the whole procedure. It is the moment when we finally realize whether the existing desire of the customer to make a purchase has been altered to a real need. This will be obvious if the customer asks us the following questions:

1. What is the product's price?
2. What is the cost of the enrolment?
3. What is it necessary to become a subscriber?
4. How much does it cost?
5. Is there any kind of arrangement that you offer?
6. How can I have it?
7. How many days are needed for the   product's delivery? etc.

This is exactly - like external sales - the "zero point", the time when we realize that the person standing opposite to us is really interested in our product or service. Our immediate reaction is:

A) To take the order form or the application forms or the forms including the modes of payment concerning our product while saying that:

1.   The procedure needed for someone to become a subscriber is very simple; we simply complete this application form...

2.   The mode of payment concerning the product is very simple...

3.   There are two modes of payment, cash or by cheque...

4.   The present arrangement is the following...

Finally, we conclude decisively:

1.   Do you want to see the whole procedure in practice?

2.   Shall we proceed?

3.   I will need your personal data...

4.   Let's begin with your name...

5.   Is your full name Michael Carroll?

6.   Tell me to which data you wish the invoice to be issued...

7.   Is it convenient for you to receive the product tomorrow? Etc.

B) Or we simply send him to the cash.

Just like in case of external sales, the person included in the capacity during that particular day will finally proceed to the purchase. The person that is not included in the capacity that particular day will not make any questions - in most cases - regarding the price of our product or service as well as the way he can obtain them.

Tips

1. There is a very simple technique in the cases of objects' selling which is applied when we realize that a potential customer has not formed yet an opinion about what he is looking for. In fact, we lead the customer to choose among three products each time. In case we want to present a forth product, we take back a product that we have already shown to the customer. According to researches, the customer can make a better choice if he has to choose among three products. This is a very effective technique that leads to immediate results since we lead the customer to decide what he is exactly looking for. We refer to the features of each product separately as well as to the benefits each product offers to the customer and finally we conclude by saying: "Which one do you finally prefer?" A second alternative will be to propose to our customer

which product will better meet his own needs. It is very important that we make a suggestion in a confident and decisive way and that this suggestion represents our real opinion. In most cases, the customer through this simple technique, proceeds to a purchase.

2. The customer, although he is really interested in buying, may need some time in order to complete his purchase or he may complete it another day. In most cases, the customer will come to us to complete his final purchase.

3. In case of internal sales, we have to understand that our role is active and not at all passive. In this kind of procedure, we are the main protagonist and our role is not a simple help towards potential customers. If we understand this and participate actively by constantly applying the procedure we have learnt as well as by leading our customer to all stages, then we will take full advantage of the capacity characterizing those people that come to our store every day and we will see that our sales are highly increased.

4. We never forget our basic principle: "Firstly, we sell the product to ourselves, and then we sell it

to the customer". If we were the customer, would we feel nice with what they tell us? Would we feel that they pay attention to us and give us the recognition we deserve? Are they kind to us since we have chosen their store to make a purchase? Do they participate actively in the sale procedure or are they indifferent for our choices? If we feel satisfied about our presence as well as the whole procedure then the customer will feel the same too and you have to be sure that he will return to us so as to finish his purchase, in case he has not already done it.

5. We can increase sales through supplementary sales. In other words we suggest a second item that is supplementary to what our customer has just bought and thus we can increase sales towards the same customers. For example, if the customer has bought a shirt we can suggest him to buy a tie. In case the customer has bought a pair of trousers, we can suggest him to buy a blouse too. Try it. It will be successful!

Telemarketing Procedure

The last sale procedure is made through the phone and it is the so-called telemarketing. Benefits concerning this kind of sales procedure are the low cost along with a sort of communication with a large number of people in a very limited time period. In fact, telemarketing is divided into two fields.

The first field has to do with the fixing of arrangements among the seller or sellers and the potential customers of a region while the second is the so-called distant sale which is directly addressed through the phone to the potential customers.

The telemarketing policy

In both cases, our policy is to cover as much of the capacity characterizing the total of potential customers with whom we will get in contact that day as possible by making as many phone calls as possible. In any case, we aim at making phone calls to those customers related to our scope.

Therefore, we use some tools such as the telephone directory or some publications in a simple or digital form containing all enterprises of the country per type of activity, region etc so as to have access to all enterprises that we are interested in.

The telemarketing stages
Case One (Arranging an appointment)

In this case, we intend - as we have already stated - to arrange as many appointments as possible, placing them in a time period of a day until a week from the day we have arranged the appointments.

Example: Good morning. My name is Andrew Anteon and I am calling you from the X company working on.... I would like to talk to the person responsible for supplies or to the company's manager. At the present time, we have a new product.... which offers you up to 15% reduction in comparison to all conventional products that exist at this time being in the market. Therefore, I would like to arrange an appointment with you. Is it convenient for you if we arrange an appointment on Monday morning at 12.00?

Thus we are specific, we show exactly what we offer and what we ask for and we do not waste the customer's time.

Case Two (Distant selling)

In this second case, namely telephone sales, we put in practice the procedure of external sales, in other words the procedure including our entrance and introduction - who we are and what we sell - sampling and the final stage as if the customer were next to us and we talked to him.

Since we do not have an immediate visual contact with the potential customer and we are not aware of his reactions, the most important clue in distant sales is to attract his attention just from the beginning.

Example: Good morning Mr. Hall. My name is Chris Smith and I am calling you from the X company that is a telephone company. At the present time, we have some very cheap programs that can offer you up to 20% reduction regarding your phone bill. Are you one of our subscribers Mr. Hall?

Thus, we attract the customer's interest just from the beginning while we predispose him so as to keep up with the rest of the sale procedure.

Tips

1. In telemarketing, in comparison with all the other sales types, we need but we also can have a "compass", in other words a kind of written script that we will have in front of us during our

conversation with the potential customer. This will help us not to forget the main points that we should underline and it will be our guide during the whole procedure.

2. In telemarketing, it is also important not to forget the basic rule: "Firstly, we sell a product to ourselves and then we sell it to the customer". If we feel satisfied by the whole procedure and the way we try to sell our product, the same the potential customer will feel and our chances to reach a final positive result are far more increased.

3. We always ask to talk to the right person - the company's manager - or if this is not possible, with the person who is responsible for the company's supplies or orders.

4. We never forget the power and usefulness of smiling. Especially in case of telemarketing where the customer forms an image through the phone and there is no visual contact, smiling as well the expression depicted in our voice are necessary so as the customer can feel familiar with us.

Chapter Three

The 22 Basic Principles of
Professional Sales

According to a new sales perception as we analyzed it in the former chapter, we do not sell, we simply help the others to buy. Hence, by taking in advance the capacity of all people that we see every day and by putting into practice the sale procedure in all cases, each one of us can be a seller.

Thus, we aim not only at selling every day but also at learning to take 100% advantage of the capacity and being stable at it by having the best possible results.

To achieve the above mentioned, we learn and implement the 22 Basic Principles of Sales that are presented in this chapter. These principles can make us from simple people working on sales to Professional Sellers. They are all important and can be implemented in all types of sales.

First Basic Principle: Communication

An experienced Professional Seller that has spent both effort and time to reach the point where he is at the present time, realizes that in fact behind the sale procedure itself lies something else: communication. The sale procedure cannot exist without communication. The person who knows how to communicate with people can also make sales.

The first and most important step for a sale to be achieved is "communication" between the seller and the buyer. Since the seller is the one who is mainly interested in reaching a positive result, he is the one who should aim at communicating with the buyer.

How will this happen? By listening to the customer. Maybe, the most important disadvantage of a person who would like to work on sales is not to listen to the one that stands in front of him. Of course, the seller should listen to him in an active way, he should try to understand his needs and not only listen to the customer passively.

To achieve a sale, there should be a "dialogue" between the seller (entrance - presentation - features - benefits - profit etc) and the buyer (questions - objections etc). Hence, we give the customer the opportunity and we urge him to express himself so as we understand what exactly he is looking for and how we can offer him what he wants to buy. The seller should have the control of the dialogue by keeping a balance between the two parties. Thus, before we start selling we should learn how to communicate.

Second Basic Principle: Trust

Nowadays, the customer requires two things from his cooperators: respect and trust. He requires respect for what he is and trust towards the person that has chosen to cooperate with. We should try to gain the customer's trust. Let's not forget that before the customer, the seller represents the company he works for. He is the person through whom the customer will form a particular opinion regarding the company the seller represents and whether the customer could manage to trust it for a successful collaboration. Thus, the seller reflects the company to the customer: in order to trust our company, he should first of all trust us.

Since trust is a very important issue nowadays, we have to be careful and honest about what we say. We should be able to put into practice whatever we promise. In case a problem comes up, we should be there whenever the customer asks for our help and we should do our best in order to find a solution.

59

Third Basic Principle: Respect Towards the Customer, His Reactions and His Knowledge.

In fact, our potential customer does not always react the way we wish. Many times - under strict work conditions and because of the daily routine - his reactions maybe abrupt, nervous and sometimes ironic. We should not forget that modern man has learnt to be fortified behind a cruel personality so as to be able to avoid a great number of persons who are not worthy of his trust. In this case, we should be calm and polite and we should try to calm all spirits.

Also, the customer may not be aware of the product that we sell. Moreover, all customers are not of the same awareness or of the same educational level. So, we have to explain to our customer everything all over the beginning in a polite, tolerant way and without resenting if he cannot understand everything right away. Hence, we have to show respect towards the customer's knowledge, reactions and personality.

Forth Basic Principle: To Be Aware of the Product

The main thing is that the product will be sold eventually by its own. The seller is the person who will talk about the product, its features and benefits, in other words what its components are, when it was made, to whom it concerns or not, what the customer will gain if he uses this particular service or what the benefits are in case it is a kind of product and of course what its price and value are.

Does the customer have to pay it immediately or is there some kind of arrangement? If there is a kind of arrangement, how much is the deposit, how much do installments cost etc. Finally, what are the most important features of the product against the existing competition and how can they become benefits for the customer?

We have to know everything about the product we sell. We should learn every single detail it has to do with it. Would we buy this product? Would we be subscribers to the service we sell to others? These two questions are very critical and we have to give an answer if we want to be honest both to ourselves and to our potential customers. A Professional Seller is the first person to buy the product he sells or the service he offers. Thus, he becomes the customer and sees the benefits or profit he can have when he decides to buy either the product or the service he sells.

Thus, after dealing with his product as a customer, the seller is ready to answer to every possible question and he is prepared to give a real answer concerning every single detail regarding the product, a fact that comes from his complete knowledge about the product as well as his own experience as a customer.

Fifth Basic Principle: To Be Aware of Our Company

In order to be successful as Professional Sellers we have to know everything concerning the company we represent. What is our company? Is it a large company or a small one? Does it count many years in this particular field or has it been recently established? Has it got many clients or a restricted number of customers due to bad policies? What are its positive features against the existing competition? Does it work in a regional, a national or a global level?

Has our company proved its power all these years of operation? Do we have examples of satisfied customers? Is the company's reaction immediate in case it comes up a problem during the sale procedure or after it? Does the company support its sellers when it is needed? Does it support the customer when it is needed? Is the company interested in satisfying the customer or does it aim exclusively at gaining profit from him? Does marketing support sales in its own way? Is it used to make promotions with the help of advertising?

All these questions stated above may not concern us in a direct way but they are very important

63

for our customer in order to evaluate our company. In any case, we have to be ready to give an answer.

Sixth Basic Principle: To Be Aware of the Concept of Competition

In our world, competition existed, still exists and it will always continue to exist in every human activity. Many people believe nowadays that the bigger the competition is concerning a product, the less the possibilities are to sell it. This opinion is a huge mistake. Do you know which products are the most difficult to sell? Those that are characterized by the less competition!! Why? Because competition is equal to free advertising.

Thus, competition does not play any important role. It does not even matter how many sellers have already spoken to our potential customer. The only thing that seriously matters is who we are and how professional we are regarding our job, in other words if we enter an enterprise in a professional way, if we deal with each one of our customers that enter our store in a professional way and eventually, if we show enough professionalism so as our potential customer can trust us.

Let me tell you a secret: when you enter the place of your potential customer you should think that you are the first person who meets the customer to talk to him about this particular product. In fact, you are the first person: the customer may have heard all these things many times before but he had not heard them from you.

Consequently, we should not be scared of competition but we should be aware of it. What are the other companies of the same field? It is helpful to carry out a research concerning this issue so as to form our own opinion regarding competition in our field. Do we know all positive features of our company against our competitors? Do we belong to a big or small enterprise of our field? If we belong to a small company and in case our customer asks us, do we know all advantages charactering our company against a bigger enterprise?

Let's be more precise. A small enterprise:

1. Pays greater attention to each one of its customers.

2. It is more flexible. We discuss about something at this present moment and it can be implemented immediately and not in a week.

3. It is more adaptable meaning that in case there is an initial agreement with a customer, everything is more positive in the future.

4. It is more personal. Prices can be adapted to each customer's demands.

5. There is an immediate delivery of the products.

If we belong to a big enterprise, our strong points can be the following:

1. Our company's power along with its extended clientele shows us that many people trust our company.

2. Advertising as well as marketing of a big company enforce its products. This means that the customer knows its products quite or very well.

3. Long-term cooperation: such a big company inspires safety for a long- term cooperation.

4. There is the possibility of lower prices in the company's products compared to the average characterizing its competitors and this is due to the company's power.

Thus, in any case regardless of the competition and the other companies existing in this particular field, we always pay attention to the positive features of our company so as to gain our customer's trust. Always remember: the market out there is really huge. Saturation will never happen. In case there is saturation of a product, sooner or later other similar products will come up. Human needs never end because this is exactly what human nature is.

Seventh Basic Principle: Have Faith in Yourself

Trusting ourselves and what we are as human beings is the most important equipment we have in life. Losing faith is one of the most important reasons that cause most people fail in every field, in every era and in every society. We should trust ourselves. We should have faith that we can succeed. Having faith in ourselves, our abilities and in the fact that we are capable of succeeding in everything we have decided to do, despite all difficulties and obstacles we face, is the most important element that can make a human of every era to succeed.

No matter how good we are at something, how genius we turn to be, if we do not believe that we can do it, we will never reach success. There are many people with great talents and abilities that could never manage to step forward because they did not have faith in themselves and their capabilities.

Every day, innumerable books and articles are written in the whole world about this particular issue as well as countless seminars and lectures take place worldwide concerning the importance of having faith in ourselves and the evolution of our lives. According to most religions and sciences, having faith in ourselves is a primitive element of our lives.

There will always be obstacles. There will always be competition in everything we do in our life. We will have to face difficulties in any field we choose to work. Many people will quit. Some others will "be thrown" out of the job they have decided to do. But this will never happen to us. We will go on because we believe we are able to make it.

Eighth Basic Principle: Have Faith in Our Company

We should have faith in the company we represent in order to promote it. The customer will not have confidence in our company unless we believe in it as well. There will always be problems, obscurities and malfunctions in any company. We should not worry about it provided we think that all this happens within normal limits.

Thus, we have to strongly believe in our company so as this faith can be transferred to the customer as well. We have to build strong binds of cooperation with our superiors, our cooperators and our employers. At work, we have to behave in a professional way and cooperate with others so as to reach positive results.

We should be the first to believe that any problem which will come up will be definitely solved. We should be the first to believe that our company can support its customer when it is necessary. We have also to be sure that our company is honest and can meet market's demands. If we are not sure about all these, we had better work for another company.

Ninth Basic Principle: Have Faith in the Product to Be Sold

As weird as it seems, we have to realize that having faith in what we sell is really important. We have to believe that the product or service we sell has positive effects to the customer. We should be the first to believe that the customer will have benefits from that purchase. We have to express to our customer in our own way that he will gain profit by this purchase.

Thus, having faith in our product or service as well as in the benefits that will offer to the customer will lead us to a successful sale. Let's not have illusions. Every product and every service nowadays has both strong and weak points. This does not mean that we have to focus on the weak features of a product or service since in that case there would seize too exist any sale. We have to concentrate on the fact that strong points of a product or service should exceed all weak ones so as the value of this particular product is high.

We have to believe that appreciation for a product is based on the fact that its benefits are more important than its weak points as well as on the fact that these benefits are considered to be important for those persons that will buy this particular product.

71

Tenth Basic Principle: A Stable Psychology

As we have already seen in the first chapter, according to Pareto's principle, the 80% of our sales will come from the 20% of our customers. Alternatively, the 80% of our sales will come from the 20% of our time. What does this practically mean? This means that time in sales does not pass by uniformly or even better, results in sales do not appear in a uniform way. It is possible that throughout a day we will not have a single result although we apply the whole sale procedure correctly and carefully. But, during the last hours we may manage to make the sales of the whole day.

Hence, a seller has to compromise with the lack of uniformity concerning time. He should maintain a stable psychology, keeping his self-confidence as well as his faith that he will definitely reach positive results. Hence, a stable psychology along with a positive attitude plays an important role in our long-term, stable performance. This is the fundamental element that characterizes successful sellers.

Moreover, as far as sales are concerned, each day is a different day. No matter what happened yesterday, it is not sure that it will also happen today. If all these influence our psychology, we will lose the game. If we become short - tempered because some people behave in a negative way towards us, this will have general effects on us. Everything is a matter of a stable psychology.

Eleventh Basic Principle: Professionalism

Since we have become Professional Sellers, we have to act in a professional way. Professionalism begins with our appearance, in other words with the way we present ourselves in front of a potential customer, the tools and means we use during a professional appointment and finally, a correct behavior towards our customer such as our exact arrival at our appointment as well as the control of a smooth conversation without misconducts with our potential customer. Let's be more analytical.

Appearance

The way we appear both to ourselves and to our customers is a fundamental factor for our psychology. Haven't you noticed how a new cloth that makes us look five years younger can change our psychology? Thus, a right and careful appearance can help us to change our psychology.

Our clothing should give off both professionalism and tastiness and we have to adapt it to the target group we address to. For example, if we are sellers at a department store with female or male clothing, a careful appearance will also point out the clothing we sell. In case we are external sellers and we address to directors of our city's enterprises, then is necessary to wear a suit along with a tie since this kind of clothing will give us the necessary professionalism that our potential customers have to make sure we have.

In case we address to the super markets of our region, we will not reject a more casual outfit keeping at the same time all general rules. In any case, cleanness is a prerequisite. A shaved face along with cut nails, shiny shoes and clean clothes give us the necessary self-confidence so as to start our day and make our customer trust us.

Tools used in professional sales

A professional seller uses specific tools which we should never forget. Some of these tools are our purse or our briefcase, our dossiers with leaflets of the product or service we offer, a pen, a calculator for all calculations needed, a notebook and of course a notebook containing the application forms or the order voucher. Moreover, we never forget our professional card.

All those things stated above should be placed in a right way inside our briefcase or our purse so as to be easily used. Hence, we are able to meet in a direct way all demands concerning the presentation of our product without having to search where we have put all these things. We never forget that details make the difference. In case we have arranged an appointment concerning an important project with the manager of an enterprise, it is recommended to have our tablet or laptop ready to use.

The right behavior towards our customer

1. We never keep our customer waiting for us. In case we have arranged an appointment at a specific hour with a potential customer or a customer we have already met and we think that we will not manage to be on time, we call him and inform him that we will be a little late for our appointment. If we know beforehand that because of our schedule we cannot fix an appointment at a specific hour with our customer, we tell him that we will come by between for example 3.30 and 4.00 pm. Thus, we are more flexible and our customer can make a better arrangement of his own schedule.

2. When we eventually appear to our appointment, we undertake to carry out a calm conversation with our customer during which we have to be careful so as the whole conversation is

concentrated on our main issue, namely the sale procedure. We should also make sure that the conversation is not deviated through personal characterizations that may be due to the customer's aggressive attitude towards us or the reverse. In any case, we should always have the feeling that we have the control of the situation and that we handle smoothly the whole conversation.

3. In case of internal sales, we do not keep our customer waiting for a long time and we help him right away.

Twelfth Basic Principle: Planning

There are people who naturally have learnt to plan everything in their lives. On the other hand, there are those who do not know what planning means and therefore they act spontaneously and many times in an impulsive way. Both human types need planning in sales. The first are the lucky ones since planning is a natural feature for them while the second have to discover planning and put it into practice.

Planning is necessary in sales and our time is something that needs to be planned. As we have already mentioned above, time in sales "passes by" in a different way in comparison to other professions. Thus, we have to learn how to plan our time, our appointments and our meetings.

We have to allocate the time we devote to each one of our clients properly so as to manage to meet all of them. Every morning we should make the plan of the day: where we are going and how, with whom we are going to get in contact and how many appointments or meetings we have arranged. Of course, we have to keep this schedule strictly.

Thirteenth Basic Principle: Learning

The path of learning is a safe way of development that leads us to success. In sales, constant learning is important. It broadens our mind and offers us new tools in order to reach our goals. Thus, learning can be achieved in the following ways:

Through books, various visual and acoustic means and through the internet

We live in an astonishing era for human beings. For the first time, every one of us can learn everything on every topic he is interested in. Before us, there is a huge, worldwide library: the internet. We have access to all experiences and knowledge of experts that have already worked on the topic we are interested in studying. The Internet surrounded by stacks of books and other visual-acoustic means that have been created all these years on the field of sales can give us a great advantage. It's an important benefit that if we take advantage of it, we are heading towards learning.

Hence, our priority is to page through all of them, explore them and learn from all this accumulated knowledge and experience, something that would normally take us decades to acquire it on our own.

Through training

Training in sales is both important and necessary, not only because we put in practice all these things that we have read but also because it is our first step towards action. It is the transfer of theory to action. Moreover, it supports our belief that not only is there people who work in the field of sales but also they do their job pretty well.

Experience and advice offered by our instructors will always be useful while we work as sellers. In large companies, new entrants on sales receive training during several months before the company decides to trust them completely. This kind of training is done in the following ways:

1. Through seminars concerning sale techniques, various ways of communication with the customer etc.

2. Through playing roles. Participants play the roles of both the seller and the customer and with the help of video recording they can study in detail their behavior as if they worked under actual conditions.

3. On the job training. The seller visits customers under the supervision of a more experienced seller and learns with his help.

Through our mistakes

Maybe it is hard for us to realize that all mistakes we make both in sales and in life, are not in fact "mistakes" in a strict sense of this term. They are simple acts that refill our knowledge with new data. However, we perceive those acts as mistakes since they provoke at the same time something painful: pain or a feeling of failure. If we managed to release these acts from all feelings they provoke to us (joy, pain etc.), we would realize that our acts simply provoke results.

If results are positive for us, we simply repeat the act that provoked them in the future. If results are not positive for us, we simply avoid repeating this particular act. If, during a meeting we have with a customer, we make a "mistake" - an act that simply does not bring a positive result to us - the only think we have to do in the future is not to repeat this particular act.

Thus, we feed our brain with all these new data concerning this particular act and we proceed. Through this procedure, our subconscious along with our memory will gradually reject all our "mistakes" - in other words our acts that do not bring a positive result to us - and they will keep all those acts that lead us only to positive results.

Fourteenth Basic Principle: Self-Improvement

Hence, the natural result of learning is our self-improvement which plays a really important role concerning our improvement firstly as sellers and generally speaking as human beings. Is self-improvement necessary? Yes, it is. Because the more we improve as persons, the more easily we can deal with all everyday situations.

We realize that all those things we considered to be insuperable, in fact they are not. We have simply not found the way to overcome them. Thus, self-improvement as a natural evolution of constant learning is the path that can lead us to the greatest levels of our professional performance.

Fifteenth Basic Principle: Self-Discipline

Self- discipline!! What a strict word. It refers to the discipline of ourselves! How important self-discipline is - not only concerning the field of sales but also in life - cannot be described in the pages of a single book. Self-discipline is the means through which we will try to put into practice all we have learnt so far. This will happen every day and it is not an easy procedure.

Self-discipline refers to an intentional control of our behavior in all situations that we have to deal with on a daily basis by putting into practice all knowledge we have gained, aiming at a particular result as well as at our improvement. Self-discipline is more difficult than discipline. Discipline towards persons and situations is imposed by others while self-disciplined is imposed by us. This requires a strong character along with experience and knowledge.

However, self-discipline has to fight a big enemy, the "daily routine". Daily routine shatters self-discipline. It disorganizes and extinguishes it. Therefore, we need a reason that will keep awake us every day. We need something to remind us every day who we are and what we have to do.

We need to have a "Goal" and a "Vision".

Sixteenth Basic Principle: Goal Setting

Sale is equal to goals. Goal setting in sales is so important that if we had to choose to put into practice one of all principles stated above, I would choose that one. Why goals in sales are so important? Because they are equal to motivation and motivation means action. The power of goals is huge. When we set specific goals, we tend to step towards them.

Goals set in sales should be simple, measurable and realistic. They aim at motivating the person that will accept them as well as rewarding him as soon as he reaches those targets. Goals may be temporal - daily, weekly, monthly, semester, annual etc - or quantitative - targets set for a particular number of sales or production - or they can be a combination of the above two categories.

A conscious Professional Seller should first and foremost set goals to himself and he should try every day to reach them and surpass them. In case targets are set by superiors, then:

1. They should be set in cooperation with the seller.
2. Goals should be feasible and realistic.
3. The seller should be bound to reach those goals.

4. His superiors should also be bound to give a reward to the seller provided he reaches the goals.

Seventeenth Basic Principle: Have a Vision

It is true: in sales we need to have a vision, a lifetime vision. Sales are not a simple procedure so as to make a living. It is something far more important. It is a fight against ourselves, our fears, our insecurities, against all these things that terrify us and prevent us from dreaming that we can change our lives and obtain everything we want to. Having a vision means having hope for a better life.

The sale procedure will definitely lead us to self-improvement and will offer us new possibilities, either on a professional level through our distinction as Professional Sellers and our promotion in our company as well as the creation of our own enterprise or on a personal level through the improvement of our relationship with others. That is why we need to have a vision, so as to remind us that someday we will be successful and to lighten our way towards success.

Eighteenth Basic Principle: Focus on Results and Have Passion for Victory

It does not matter whether you come from a high or low social class. It does not matter whether you studied Business Administration or you have an M.B.A. It does not even matter whether you are a high school graduate. The only thing that does matter in Professional Sales is your ability to reach results along with your passion for victory. That is the only important thing that proves your abilities.

The seller is a winner both in sales and in life. Thus, your passion for everyday victory, again and again as well as your ability to transform your daily routine, experience, success and failure into results are those things that will offer you a reward as far as your profession is concerned.

Nineteenth Basic Principle: The Reward

The most important advantage concerning those people who do this fascinating job is the reward. There is no sale without reward. First of all, there is a moral reward. The fact that the seller is acknowledged by his colleagues, his employers, his own customers and general speaking by his environment is very important and gives him the courage to go on.

Then, there is a material reward. The money reward paid to a Professional Seller is usually defined by the system "Wage - Percentage - Bonus". Sales form a field that brings in high payments in comparison with the average of other professions. This happens because a seller's payment is respective to the production he manages to make. The more the production is, the higher the payment will be.

All the above mentioned can also lead to the reverse rule according to which "when there is no satisfactory payment, sales cannot be numerous!"

Twentieth Basic Principle: Offering Help After Sale

"We never forget our clients so as not to be forgotten by them". This is another basic rule of sales which many of us have learnt through a difficult way. The procedure of sales does not end by signing an application form, a contract, an order of a potential customer, a purchase of our product or our service. In fact, this is when real sale begins.

The fact of keeping our customer satisfied and ensuring that he will be one of our constant customers is even more difficult and it should be our priority from now on. Thus, we have to visit our customer frequently and be ready to help him in every problem that may appear. The "after sales service" is a very important factor ensuring that the same customer will repeat a purchase again and again and that he will remain satisfied by our work.

Twenty First Basic Principle: Same Act - Different Subjects

There is an erroneous perception that is widespread in the business market according to which a seller can only sell this kind of products or service that have already sold in the past. In other words, he needs to have the so-called "work experience" regarding the field on which he wishes to work.

As a seller, I have worked on three completely different fields: books and publications, drinks commerce and telecommunications. In other words I have worked on two products and one kind of service. They are three complete different fields with different features, addressing different target groups: three different fields but the same procedure. Nothing really changes.

We learn as many things as we can about the field we work on and we proceed with a preparatory work. Then, we put into practice all basic principles concerning sales, we carefully repeat the whole sale procedure and finally we get our results. In market there are too many products and services but there is only one procedure concerning professional sales.

Twenty Second Basic Principle: Action

Yes, action!! Get up right now and decide to work on sales. Get in action. Leave all complaints for the others. Grab your bag, put into it all things concerning the products or services you want to sell and get out in the large and open market that waits for you. The market waits for you to sample your products or services, to discuss, to be rejected, to make sales and money.

If you knew how many people are ready to change their supplier at this moment, how many are ready to see new offers, to look for new products and services so as to raise both their ego and lifestyle, you would not miss any time at all. Action is the crowning point of all principles we have learnt so far in the present book. Knowledge has no value at all if there is no action, namely the application of knowledge so as to reach the desirable results.

Conclusion

Nowadays, modern seller does not need to convince anyone. He does not have to "manage" or "deal with" any objections of any potential customer. By learning all sale techniques and putting them into practice every day, he takes full advantage of every day capacity and thus he makes purchases and helps modern people to do what they love to do since their childhood: to buy constantly wherever they are so as to confirm themselves and improve their lifestyle on a daily basis while they try every day to adapt in a society that constantly changes, characterized by an endless consumerism as a way of living.

By assimilating all basic principles concerning sales, the seller makes a step forward. He becomes a Professional Seller, a profession that is in great demand worldwide regarding world enterprises. It is a profession that offers great earnings, wide recognition and distinction to most Professional Sellers and most of all the ability to manage themselves as well as all situations and relations with others.

However, before we proceed with the application of all principles and techniques included in the present book, we should wonder: Are we REALLY interested in sales? You are the only person that can answer this question which will finally determine your development in this fascinating profession. Good luck!!

Index

About the Author

Christos Stilianidis is a modern professional seller and businessman. He has his own business and he has already made sales to hundreds of people and enterprises. He writes books and carries out seminars concerning sales in his efforts to initiate more people to this unique profession.

For further information please visit:

www.win-on-sale.com

How This Book Was Made

This book was formatted in Microsoft Word. PDF files were produced and processed with Adobe Acrobat Pro. The text font is 10-point Georgia. The chapter headings are in 12-point Georgia. The cover was produced with CreateSpace's free Cover Creator software. All copies of this book are produced by CreateSpace.